PRENTICE HALL *Keys to Success* QUICK REVIEW

If you are not a current *Keys to Success* adopter, we want to gain your insight on this edition!

We are so excited about the upcoming 5th edition of *Keys to Success* that we have provided you with a "sneak peek" at Chapter 4, *Critical, Creative, and Practical Thinking: Solving Problems and Making Decisions.*

Tell us what you think! Simply answer the following questions, send in this completed form, and we will send you a complimentary copy of Robert Sternberg's *Successful Intelligence* in return.

Be sure to include the following information:

Professor name: _____

School name: _____

Mailing address: _____

Email address: _____ Phone: _____

1. What is the title of the student success text you are currently using? What is the annual enrollment for your course?

2. Who takes your student success course and what are the goals of the course?

3. What topics do you cover in your course? What topics do you struggle most with?

4. Please examine this sample chapter. How does the coverage in our text help to address the goals in your course? Which features do you feel would benefit your students and why?

5. Examine the activities in this sample chapter. In what ways will they provide your students with opportunities to practice new skills?

6. Based on this sample chapter, would you like to see a complimentary review copy of the text so you may consider it for your course? Why or why not?

Please fax, mail, or email this information to Tyra Poole, Senior Marketing Coordinator
445 Hutchinson Avenue, 4th Floor, Columbus, OH 43235 • tyra.poole@pearsoned.com • fax: 614-841-3702
You will receive a complimentary copy of Sternberg's *Successful Intelligence* for your feedback. Please allow time for processing upon receipt.

Keys to Success

BUILDING SUCCESSFUL INTELLIGENCE

for College, Career, and Life

FIFTH EDITION

Carol Carter

Joyce Bishop

Sarah Lyman Kravits

PEARSON

Prentice
Hall

Upper Saddle River, New Jersey
Columbus, Ohio

Vice President and Publisher: Jeffery W. Johnston
Senior Acquisitions Editor: Sande Johnson
Assistant Editor: Erin Anderson
Production Editor: Holcomb Hathaway
Design Coordinator: Diane C. Lorenzo
Cover Designer: Jeff Vanik
Cover Photos: SuperStock, PhotoDisk
Interior Design: Aerocraft Charter Art Service
Production Manager: Pamela D. Bennett
Director of Marketing: Ann Castel Davis
Marketing Manager: Amy Judd

Photo Credits:
pp. vii, 1, 4 provided by photo subjects. All other photos from
Corbis, PhotoDisk, EyeWire, Dynamic Graphics, and Hemera

Pearson Prentice Hall™ is a trademark of Pearson Education, Inc.
Pearson® is a registered trademark of Pearson plc
Prentice Hall® is a registered trademark of Pearson Education, Inc.

Pearson Education Ltd.
Pearson Education Australia Pty. Limited
Pearson Education Singapore Pte. Ltd.
Pearson Education North Asia Ltd.
Pearson Education Canada, Ltd.
Pearson Educación de Mexico, S. A. de C.V.
Pearson Education–Japan
Pearson Education Malaysia Pte. Ltd.

10 9 8 7 6 5 4 3 2 1
ISBN 0-13-170368-4

Our Mission Statement

Our mission is to help students know and believe in themselves, successfully retain and use what they learn, and take advantage of resources and opportunities. With these abilities, we are confident that all students can achieve their goals, become lifelong learners, build fruitful and satisfying relationships with others, and experience the challenges and rewards that make life meaningful.

Foreword

Everyone's experience in college is different. My experience was not that of a traditional student because I volunteered for four years of military service before going to college full time. The Marine Corps gave me discipline and instilled in me the motivation I needed to continue my education. By the time I had finished my enlistment, I had also finished my freshman year at the University of South Carolina.

The time I took to serve our country also gave me the opportunity to decide what type of college atmosphere best suited my needs. In the end, I chose to attend a small university with close ties to the businesses in Denver. The information in *Keys to Success* was important to my college education. While acting as student editor on this book, I learned how to be a better student, employee, and person. I graduated feeling ready for the rest of my life.

I took advantage of the worksheets and personal stories by applying them to my everyday life. After working with this book, I was more inclined to take active steps toward improving my education and my ability to learn. The most important thing I learned in college is, in fact, how to learn. I have a goal to learn throughout my lifetime. I want my life to be a series of new lessons about my profession and myself.

Someone once told me that a college education can be valued by the amount of effort the student puts into it. Anyone can go to class, take notes, and pass the tests. In my experience, the students who succeed in the long term make every assignment a learning challenge. I encourage you to take advantage of every opportunity to learn. Your efforts and dedication to learning are in direct relation to your degree of happiness and success in college, career, and life.

Best Wishes,

Dylan Lewis

UNIVERSITY OF COLORADO, DENVER

Preface

Since the last edition of *Keys to Success,* we have focused our energies and research on the following question: How can students get the most out of college and use what they learn to achieve their goals in an ever-changing world? We found an important answer in the concept of successful intelligence, developed by psychologist Robert Sternberg.[1]

This book builds successful intelligence

Successful people, says Sternberg, are more than their IQ score. Focus on the two most important parts of Sternberg's message and you can change your approach to education in a way that will maximize your learning and *life success.*

One: *Successful intelligence gives you tools to achieve important goals.* Successful intelligence goes beyond doing well on tests (analytical thinking). Only by combining that analytical skill with the ability to come up with innovative ideas (creative thinking) and the ability to put ideas and plans to work (practical thinking) will you get where you want to go.

Two: *Intelligence can grow.* The intelligence you have when you are born does not stay the same for the rest of your life. You can build and develop your intelligence in the same way that you can build and develop physical strength or flexibility.

Every chapter of *Keys to Success* helps you to build successful intelligence. How?

- *Chapter coverage:* The theme is introduced in Chapter 1 and covered in more detail in the thinking chapter (Chapter 4). Successful intelligence concepts are referenced throughout all chapters of the text.
- *In-text exercises:* Three exercises within the chapter text—"Get Analytical," "Get Creative," and "Get Practical"—develop each skill in the context of the chapter material and your personal needs.
- *Synthesis exercise:* At the end of each chapter, the "Putting It All Together" exercise gives you an opportunity to combine all three skills and apply them toward a meaningful task.

This book connects you with the ideas and experiences of others

To help you excel in a world that is increasingly diverse, this edition of *Keys to Success* introduces the concept of *cultural competence,* using the following features:

- *Chapter-opening Q & A* highlights questions posed by actual students as they begin college. Each question is answered by another person who has had similar experiences.
- *Descriptions of real students' experiences,* often accompanied by quotes from the students, have been woven into the text in areas where they enhance the topic being discussed.
- *A focus on cultural competence,* in Chapter 9, shows the value of going beyond tolerance to actively adapt to and learn from people different from you. References to cultural competence and diversity are also woven throughout every chapter, showing how diversity is part of many aspects of school, the workplace, and personal life.
- *Personal Triumph* stories, real-life accounts of how people have overcome difficult circumstances in the pursuit of education and fulfillment, appear near the end of every third chapter. These inspiring stories motivate you to step up your personal efforts to succeed.
- *Chapter summaries* introduce a word or phrase from a language other than English

and suggest how you might apply the concept to your own life.

- *A continuing focus on multiple intelligences* highlights individual diversity and confirms that each individual has a unique way of learning, with no one way being better than another. Chapter 3 introduces and explains this concept, and subsequent chapters include grids with strategies for applying various learning styles to the chapter content.

This book provides strategies and resources that help you do your work

With successful intelligence as the foundation of this edition and cultural competence as an underlying theme, *Keys to Success* presents these learning tools and materials that will help you succeed in college and beyond:

A college primer. Because there's so much to know right off the bat, the section "Quick Start to College" appears at the beginning of this text. Quick Start helps you get a feel for the structure of your college, the people who can help you with academic and life issues, the resources available to you, and expectations from instructors, administrators, and fellow students.

Skills that prepare you for college, career, and life. The ideas and strategies that help you succeed in college also take you where you want to go in your career and personal life. The three parts of this text help you develop a firm foundation for lifelong learning.

- *Defining yourself and your goals.* Chapter 1 provides an overview of today's college experience and an opportunity to evaluate your personal starting point. Chapter 2 gets you on track with ways to manage yourself effectively, focusing on values, goal-setting strategies, time-management skills, and handling stress. Chapter 3 helps you identify complementary aspects of your learning style (your Multiple Intelligences and your Personality Spectrum profile), choose strategies that make them work for you, and begin to think about your major.
- *Developing your learning skills.* Chapter 4 puts your learning into action by exploring the concept of successful intelligence in depth,

helping you to build analytical, creative, and practical thinking skills and to put them together in order to solve problems, make decisions, and achieve goals. The next few chapters build crucial skills for the classroom and beyond—Reading and Studying (Chapter 5), Listening, Note Taking, and Memory (Chapter 6), Test Taking (Chapter 7), and Researching and Writing (Chapter 8).

- *Creating success.* Recognizing that success includes more than academic achievement, Chapter 9 focuses on developing the interpersonal and communication skills you need in a diverse society. Chapter 10 helps you to manage the stress and wellness issues that so many college students face, and Chapter 11 covers the money-management and career-planning skills you need in college and beyond. Finally, Chapter 12 helps you think expansively: What path have you traveled during the semester? What plans do you have for your future?

Skill-building exercises. Today's graduates need to be effective thinkers, team players, writers, and strategic planners. The set of exercises at the end of each chapter—"Building Skills for College, Career, and Life Success"—encourages you to develop these valuable skills and to apply thinking processes to any topic or situation:

- *Developing Successful Intelligence: Putting It All Together.* These exercises encourage you to combine your successful intelligence thinking skills and apply them to chapter material.
- *Team Building: Collaborative Solutions.* This exercise gives you a chance to interact, problem solve, and learn in a group setting, building your teamwork and leadership skills in the process.
- *Writing: Discovery Through Journaling.* This journal exercise provides an opportunity to express your thoughts and develop your writing skills.
- *Career Portfolio: Plan for Success.* This exercise helps you gather evidence of your talents, skills, interests, qualifications, and experience. The Career Portfolio exercises build on one another to form, at the end of the semester, a portfolio of information and

insights that will help you in your quest for the right career and job.

Particular help with test taking. At three places in the text, a segment called "Becoming a Better Test Taker" appears. Each segment features a test-taking topic and helps you to develop your test-taking skills throughout the semester in addition to your work on the test-taking chapter.

This book changes with your needs

As we revise, we are in constant touch with students and instructors who tell us how we can improve. From our work with students, student editors, instructors, and experts all over the country, we have made important changes to better focus this new edition on what you need to succeed now. Here's what's new:

- The text-wide theme of successful intelligence—the way to achieve goals and success through analytical, creative, and practical thinking
- A new focus in Chapter 1 on how to use and benefit from the text and its theme
- Three in-chapter exercises in each chapter—one building analytical thinking skill, one building creative thinking skill, and one building practical thinking skill
- A new first exercise at the end of each chapter—"Building Successful Intelligence: Putting It All Together"—to encourage the synthesis of successful intelligence thinking skills
- Earlier placement (in Chapter 2) of values, goal setting, time management, and basic stress management strategies
- Revision of learning styles material in Chapter 3 to more clearly delineate the two learning styles assessments and enhance their usefulness
- Extensive revision of Chapter 4—the thinking chapter—to focus on successful intelligence and how it makes problem solving and decision making happen
- Earlier placement of test-taking material (in Chapter 7) as well as in the "Becoming a Better Test Taker" segments.

- Revision of Chapter 9—the diversity chapter—to focus on cultural competence, along with added cultural references throughout the text
- New student stories included within the text to heighten relevance of the material and the reader's ability to connect to it
- Newly revised end-of-chapter exercises to increase relevance and usefulness and to help students build on what they learn throughout the semester

This book is just a start—only you can create the life of your dreams

As you work through this course and move forward toward your goals, keep this in mind: Studies have shown that when students feel that they have a fixed level of intelligence, they improve less, put less effort into their work, and have a harder time in the face of academic challenges. However, students who feel that they can become more intelligent over time are more likely to improve, tend to work harder, and handle academic challenges with more success.[2] Believe that your intelligence can grow—and use this book to develop it this semester, throughout your college experience, and afterward as you build the future of your dreams.

Students and instructors: Many of our best suggestions have come from you. Send your questions, comments, and ideas about *Keys to Success* to Carol Carter at caroljcarter@lifebound.com or call our toll-free number at 1-877-737-8510. We look forward to hearing from you, and we are grateful for the opportunity to work with you.

Notes

1. Successful intelligence concepts from Robert Sternberg, *Successful Intelligence*. New York: Plume, 1997.

2. David Glenn, "Students' Performance on Tests is Tied to Their Views of Their Innate Intelligence, Researchers Say." *The Chronicle of Higher Education*, 6/1/2004. Available: http://chronicle.com/daily/2004/06/2004060 103n.htm (June 2004).

Brief Contents

Contents

Chapter 9

RELATING TO OTHERS
Communicating in a Diverse World

Chapter 10

PERSONAL WELLNESS
Taking Care of Yourself

Chapter 11

MANAGING CAREER AND MONEY
Reality Resources

Chapter 12

CREATING YOUR LIFE
Building a Successful Future

NOTE: *Every effort has been made to provide accurate and current Internet information in this book. However, the Internet and information posted on it are constantly changing, so it is inevitable that some of the Internet addresses listed in this textbook will change.*

About the Authors

Carol Carter is founder of LifeBound, a career coaching company that offers individual coaching sessions and seminars for high school students, college students, and career seekers. She has written *Majoring in the Rest of Your Life: Career Secrets for College Students* and *Majoring in High School.* She has also co-authored *Keys to Preparing for College, Keys to College Studying, The Career Tool Kit, Keys to Career Success, Keys to Study Skills, Keys to Thinking and Learning,* and *Keys to Success.* She has taught welfare-to-work classes, team taught in the La Familia Scholars Program at the Community College of Denver, and conducted numerous workshops for students and faculty around the country. Carol is a national college and career expert and is interviewed regularly in print, on the radio, and for television news programs. In addition to working with students of all ages, Carol thrives on foreign travel and culture; she has been fortunate enough to have been a guest in more than 40 foreign countries. Please visit her website and write her at **www.lifebound.com.**

Joyce Bishop holds a Ph.D. in psychology and has taught for more than 20 years, receiving a number of honors, including Teacher of the Year for 1995 and 2000. For five years she has been voted "favorite teacher" by the student body and Honor Society at Golden West College, Huntington Beach, California, where she has taught since 1987 and is a tenured professor. She has worked with a federal grant to establish Learning Communities and Workplace Learning in her district, and she has developed workshops and trained faculty in cooperative learning, active learning, multiple intelligences, workplace relevancy, learning styles, authentic assessment, team building, and the development of learning communities. Joyce is currently teaching online and multimedia classes, and she trains other faculty to teach online in her district and region of 21 colleges. She co-authored *Keys to College Studying, Keys to Success, Keys to Thinking and Learning,* and *Keys to Study Skills.* Joyce is the lead academic of the Keys to Lifelong Learning Telecourse, distributed by Dallas Telelearning.

Sarah Lyman Kravits comes from a family of educators and has long cultivated an interest in educational development. She co-authored *Keys to College Studying, The Career Tool Kit, Keys to Success, Keys to Thinking and Learning,* and *Keys to Study Skills* and has served as Program Director for LifeSkills, Inc., a nonprofit organization that aims to further the career and personal development of high school students. In that capacity she helped to formulate both curricular and organizational elements of the program, working closely with instructors as well as members of the business community. She has also given faculty workshops in critical thinking. Sarah holds a B.A. in English and drama from the University of Virginia, where she was a Jefferson Scholar, and an M.F.A. from Catholic University.

IN THIS CHAPTER...

*you will explore answers
to the following questions:*

Critical, Creative, and Practical Thinking

SOLVING PROBLEMS AND MAKING DECISIONS

To survive and to thrive in college and beyond, you will need to use your thinking power to do more than remember formulas for a test. When problems or decisions arise on the road toward goals large and small, how can you work through them successfully? The answer lies in how you combine your analytical, creative, and practical thinking skills—in other words, how you use your successful intelligence. As you remember from Chapter 1, successful intelligence is "the kind of intelligence used to achieve important goals."[1]

Thinking, like note taking or car repair, is a skill that can be developed with practice. This chapter will help you build your ability to analyze information, come up with creative ideas, and put a practical plan into action. With these skills you can become a better thinker, problem solver, and decision maker, able to reach the goals that mean the most to you.

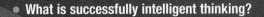

- What is successfully intelligent thinking?
- How can you improve your analytical thinking skills?
- How can you improve your creative thinking skills?
- How can you improve your practical thinking skills?
- How can you use your thinking skills to solve problems and make decisions?

How do I decide which classes I will need?

Every semester it's a challenge to figure out the classes I need. I am majoring in microbiology, but the science courses I need aren't always available. Also, I eventually want to transfer to the University of Illinois. The processes for registering and figuring out what credits will transfer seem complicated.

When I came to the States for college, only a few of my math credits transferred because the math classes I had taken in high school in Venezuela were not acceptable. My freshman year I took two algebra classes and later found out that they couldn't be applied to my major. I may want to go back to Venezuela during the summers. I've considered taking classes then, but the Venezuelan universities don't really offer my major. Do you have suggestions for what I can do to make this process more efficient?

Edhilvia Campos
Parkland Community College, Champaign, Illinois

Find an academic counselor in your field who can guide you . . .

First and foremost, hang in there. I know that things seem hard now, but your efforts will pay off. Attending college is similar to a "micro" real world. Throughout college, you will have to face problems that must be solved. I understand that you feel you wasted time and money taking certain classes. But some classes are not always transferable, and unfortunately money has to be spent to take certain courses before entering a degree program.

To prepare to transfer, find an academic counselor at the University of Illinois (preferably one in your major) who can tell you what will transfer so that you will not have to repeat or take unnecessary classes. While at Parkland, find an academic counselor in your field who can guide you toward appropriate courses for that degree, and use the undergraduate catalog to stay informed of the necessary classes for your major. Get to know the professors in your field because they can help. If some classes are not available for one semester, gather at least 8 to 10 students to voice concern about opening a section. Professors are often unaware of the demand for certain courses because students do not speak up.

If you do plan to return to Venezuela for the summer, only take courses that will apply to your degree or take some general lower-division classes that are transferable. Make sure you check with the counselors at Parkland and the University of Illinois before signing up. All in all, keep your determination alive and do not let things discourage you. Always find something valuable within each course you take because this will help you become more well rounded. Remember to think positive; this is only a "micro" real-world experience, helping to prepare you for the R-E-A-L world.

Shera Chantel Caviness
Graduate, University of Memphis

What is *successfully intelligent* thinking?

Robert Sternberg uses this story to illustrate the impact of successful intelligece:

> Two boys are walking in a forest. They are quite different. The first boy's teachers think he is smart, his parents think he is smart, and as a result, he thinks he is smart. He has good test scores, good grades, and other good paper credentials that will get him far in his scholastic life.
>
> Few people consider the second boy smart. His test scores are nothing great, his grades aren't so good, and his other paper credentials are, in general, marginal. At best, people would call him shrewd or street smart.
>
> As the two boys walk along in the forest, they encounter a problem—a huge, furious, hungry-looking grizzly bear, charging straight at them. The first boy, calculating that the grizzly bear will overtake them in 17.3 seconds, panics. In this state, he looks at the second boy, who is calmly taking off his hiking boots and putting on his jogging shoes.
>
> The first boy says to the second boy, "You must be crazy. There is no way you are going to outrun that grizzly bear!"
>
> The second boy replies, "That's true. But all I have to do is outrun you!"[2]

This story shows that successful problem solving and decision making require more than "book smarts." When confronted with a problem, using only analytical thinking put the first boy at a disadvantage. On the other hand, the second boy thought in different ways; he analyzed the situation, creatively considered the options, and took practical action. He asked and answered questions. He knew his purpose. And he lived to tell the tale.

Successfully intelligent thinking is balanced

Some tasks require only one thinking skill, or ability, at a time. You might use analytical thinking to complete a multiple-choice quiz, creative thinking to figure out how to get a paper done the same day you work a long shift, or practical thinking to put together a desk marked "some assembly required." However, when you need to solve a problem or make a decision, your analytical, creative, and practical thinking skills build upon one another to move you forward.[3] Envision it this way: Just as a pyramid needs three sides in order to stand, successful thinkers need all three thinking skills to develop the best solutions and decisions (see Key 4.1).

Each thinking skill adds an important dimension to accomplishing goals. Developing a balanced set of skills and knowing how and when to use each of them gives you more thinking power than having a strong aptitude in any one ability.[4] This kind of flexible thinking will help you connect your academic tasks to life goals—and show you where your hard work can take you (see Key 4.2).

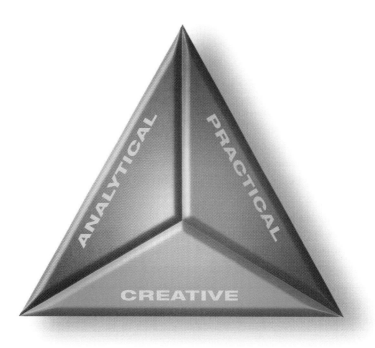

Successfully intelligent thinking means asking and answering questions

What is thinking? According to experts, it is what happens when you ask questions and move toward the answers.[5] "To think through or rethink anything," says Dr. Richard Paul, Director of Research at the Center for Critical Thinking and Moral Critique, "one must ask questions that stimulate our thought. Questions define tasks, express problems and delineate issues. . . . only students who have questions are really thinking and learning."[6]

As you answer questions, you transform raw data into information that you can use. A *Wall Street Journal* article entitled "The Best Innovations Are Those That Come From Smart Questions" relays the story of a cell biology student, William Hunter, whose professor told him that "the difference between good science and great science is the quality of the questions posed." Later, as a doctor and the president and CEO of a pharmaceutical company, Dr. Hunter asked questions about new ways to use drugs. His questions led to the development of a revolutionary product—a drug-coated coronary stent that prevents scar tissue from forming. Through seeking answers to probing questions, Dr. Hunter reached a significant goal.[7]

You use questions in order to analyze ("How bad is my money situation?"), come up with creative ideas ("What ways could I earn money?"), and apply practical solutions ("How can I get a job on campus?"). Later in the chapter, in the sections on analytical, creative, and practical thinking, you will find examples of the kinds of questions that drive each skill.

Like any aspect of thinking, questioning is not often a straightforward process. Sometimes the answer doesn't come right away. Often the answer leads to more—and more specific—questions.

Successful intelligence helps you achieve goals in any discipline.

DISCIPLINE	ANALYTICAL THINKING	CREATIVE THINKING	PRACTICAL THINKING
Behavioral Science	Comparing one theory of child development with another	Devising a new theory of child development	Applying child development theories to help parents and teachers understand and deal with children more effectively
Literature	Analyzing the development of the main character in a novel	Writing alternative endings to the novel	Using the experience of the main character to better understand and manage one's own life situations
History	Considering similarities and differences between World War I and World War II	Imagining yourself as a German citizen, dealing with economic depression after WWI	Seeing what WWI and WWII lessons can be applied to current Middle East conflicts
Sports	Analyzing the opposing team's strategy on the soccer field	Coming up with innovative ways to move the ball downfield	Using tactics to hide your strategy from an opposing team—or a competing company

Source: Adapted from Robert J. Sternberg, *Successful Intelligence.* Plume: New York, 1997, p. 149.

Successfully intelligent thinking requires knowing your purpose

In order to ask useful questions, you need to know why you are questioning. In other words, you need to define your purpose. Not knowing your purpose may lead you to ask questions that take you in irrelevant directions and waste your time. For example, if an assignment asks you to analyze the effectiveness of John F. Kennedy's foreign policy during his presidency, asking questions about his personal life may lead you off the track.

A general question can be your starting point for defining your purpose: "What am I trying to accomplish, and why?" Then, within each stage of the process, you will find more specific purposes, or sub-goals, that help you generate analytical, creative, or practical questions along the way.

Successfully intelligent thinking is yours to build

You can improve, now and throughout your life, your ability to think. Studies have shown that the brain continues to develop throughout your life if you continue to learn new things.[8] Puzzle master Nob Yoshigahara has said, "As jogging is to the body, thinking is to the brain. The more we do it, the better we become."[9]

The mini-assessments within this chapter will help you to get an idea of how you perceive yourself as an analytical, creative, and practical thinker. Every other chapter's set of *Get Analytical, Get Creative,* and *Get Practical* exercises then helps you to build your skills in those areas. Finally, the *Developing Successful Intelligence: Putting It All Together* exercises at the ends of chapters encourage you to

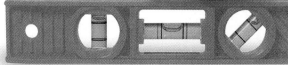

both build and combine your skills. *Your work throughout the book is geared toward building your successful intelligence.*

Begin by exploring the analytical thinking skills that you'll need in order to solve problems and make decisions effectively.

How can you improve your *analytical thinking* skills?

Analytical thinking—also known as critical thinking—is the process of gathering information, analyzing it in different ways, and evaluating it for the purposes of gaining understanding, solving a problem, or making a decision. It is as essential for real-life problems and decisions as it is for thinking through the hypothetical questions on your chemistry homework.

The first step in analytical thinking, as with all aspects of successful intelligence, is to define your purpose. What do you want to analyze, and why? Perhaps you need to analyze the plot of a novel in order to determine its structure; maybe you want to analyze your schedule in order to figure out whether you are arranging your time and responsibilities effectively.

Once you define your purpose, the rest of the analytical process involves gathering the necessary information, analyzing and clarifying the ideas, and evaluating what you've found.

Gather information

Information is the raw material for thinking. Choosing what to gather requires a careful analysis of how much information you need, how much time to spend gathering it, and whether the information is relevant. Say, for instance, that your assignment is to write a paper on one style of American jazz music. If you gathered every available resource on the topic, it might be next semester before you got to the writing stage.

Here's how you might use analysis to effectively gather information for that paper:

- Reviewing the assignment, you learn that the paper should be 10 pages and cover at least three influential musicians.
- At the library and online, you find lots of what appears to be relevant information.
- You choose a jazz movement, find five or six comprehensive pieces on it, and then select three in-depth sources on each of three musicians.

In this way you achieve a sub-goal—a selection of useful materials—on the way to your larger goal of writing a well-crafted paper.

Analyze and clarify information

Once you've gathered the information, the next step is to analyze it to determine whether the information is reliable and useful in helping you answer your questions.

Break information into parts

When analyzing information, you break information into parts and examine the parts so that you can see how they relate to each other and to information you already know. The following strategies help you break information down into pieces and set aside what is unclear, unrelated, or unimportant, resulting in a deeper and more reliable understanding.

Separate the ideas. If you are reading about the rise of the Bebop movement, you might name events that influenced it, key musicians, facts about the sound, and ideas behind it.

Compare and contrast. Look at how things are similar to, or different from, each other. You might explore how three Bebop musicians are similar in style. You might look at how they differ in what they want to communicate with their music.

Examine cause and effect. Look at the possible reasons why something happened (possible causes) and its consequences (effects, both positive and negative). You might examine the causes that led up to the Bebop sound as well as its effects on other non-jazz musical styles.

An important caution: Analyze carefully to seek out *true causes*—some apparent causes may not be actual causes (often called "false causes"). For example, events in the musical world and general society took place when the first musicians were developing the Bebop style. Some may have led directly to the new style; some may simply have occurred at the same time.

Look for themes, patterns, and categories. Note connections that arise out of how bits of information relate to one another. A theme of freedom vs. structure, for example, might emerge out of an examination of Bebop vs. swing jazz. A pattern of behavior might develop as you look at how different musicians broke off from the swing movement. Musicians with different styles might fall into the Bebop category based on their artistic goals.

Too often we enjoy the comfort of opinion without the discomfort of thought.

JOHN F. KENNEDY

Once the ideas are broken down, you can examine whether examples support ideas, separate fact from opinion, consider perspective, and investigate hidden assumptions.

Examine whether examples support ideas

When you encounter an idea or claim, examine how it is supported with examples or evidence (facts, expert opinion, research findings, personal experience, and so on). Ideas that aren't backed up with solid evidence or made concrete with examples are not useful. Be critical of the information you gather; don't take it at face value.

For example, an advertisement for a weight-loss pill, claiming that it allows users to drop a pound a day, quotes "Anne" who says that she lost 30 pounds in 30 days. The word of one person, who may or may not be telling the truth, is not adequate support. On the other hand, a claim that water once existed on Mars, backed up by measurements and photography from one of the Mars Exploration Rovers, may prove more reliable.

Distinguish fact from opinion

A *statement of fact* is information presented as objectively real and verifiable ("It's raining outside right now"). In contrast, a *statement of opinion* is a belief, conclusion, or judgment that is inherently difficult, and sometimes impossible, to verify ("This is the most miserable rainstorm ever"). Key 4.3 defines important characteristics of fact and opinion. Finding credible, reliable information with which to answer questions and come up with ideas enables you to separate fact from opinion. Even though facts may seem more solid, you can also make use of opinions if you determine that they are backed up with facts. However, it is important to examine opinions for their underlying perspectives and assumptions.

Examine perspectives and assumptions

Perspective is a characteristic way of thinking about people, situations, events, and ideas. Perspectives can be broad, such as a generally optimistic or pessimistic view of life. Or they can be more focused, such as an attitude about whether students should commute or live on campus.

Perspectives are associated with *assumptions*—judgments, generalizations, or biases influenced by experience and values. For example, the perspective that there are many different successful ways to be a family leads to assumptions such as "Single-parent homes can provide nurturing environments" and "Same-sex couples can rear well-adjusted children." Having a particular experience with single-parent homes or same-sex couples can build or reinforce a perspective.

Assumptions often hide within questions and statements, blocking you from considering information in different ways. Take this classic puzzler as an example: "Which came first, the chicken or the egg?" Thinking about this question, most people assume that the egg is a chicken egg. If you think past that assumption and come up with a new idea—such as, the egg is a dinosaur egg—then the obvious answer is that the egg came first!

Examining perspectives and assumptions is important for two reasons. First, they often affect your perception of the validity of materials you read and research. Second, your own perspectives and assumptions can cloud your interpretation of the information you encounter.

Perspectives and assumptions in information

Being able to determine the perspectives that underlie materials will help you separate (biased) from unbiased information. For example, the conclusions in two articles on federal versus state government control of

[handwritten annotation] BIASED — Leaning in a particular direction; influenced by a point of view.

OPINIONS INCLUDE STATEMENTS THAT . . .	FACTS INCLUDE STATEMENTS THAT . . .
. . . *show evaluation.* Any statement of value indicates an opinion. Words such as *bad, good, pointless,* and *beneficial* indicate value judgments. Example: "Jimmy Carter is the most successful peace negotiator to sit in the White House."	. . . *deal with actual people, places, objects, or events.* Example: "In 1978, Jimmy Carter's 13-day summit meeting with Egyptian President Anwar Sadat and Israeli Prime Minister Menachem Begin led to a treaty between the two countries."
. . . *use* **abstract** *words.* Words that are complicated to define, like *misery* or *success,* usually indicate a personal opinion. Example: "The charity event was a smashing success."	. . . *use concrete words or measurable statistics.* Example: "The charity event raised $5,862."
. . . *predict future events.* Statements that examine future occurrences are often opinions. Example: "Mr. Barrett's course is going to set a new enrollment record this year."	. . . *describe current events in exact terms.* Example: "Mr. Barrett's course has 378 students enrolled this semester."
. . . *use emotional words.* Emotions are by nature unverifiable. Chances are that statements using such words as *delightful* or *miserable* express an opinion. Example: "That class is a miserable experience."	. . . *avoid emotional words and focus on the verifiable.* Example: "Citing dissatisfaction with the instruction, 7 out of the 25 students in that class withdrew in September."
. . . *use absolutes.* Absolute **qualifiers,** such as *all, none, never,* and *always,* often point to an opinion. Example: "All students need to have a job while in school."	. . . *avoid absolutes.* Example: "Some students need to have a job while in school."

Source: Adapted from Ben E. Johnson, *Stirring Up Thinking.* New York: Houghton Mifflin, 1998, pp. 268–270.

education may differ radically if one appears in a politically conservative publication and one appears in a liberal publication. Comparing those articles will require that you understand and take into account the conservative and liberal perspectives on government's role in education.

Assumptions often affect the validity of materials you read and research. A historical Revolutionary War document that originated in the colonies, for example, may assume that the rebellion against the British was entirely justified and leave out information to the contrary. Clearly understanding such a document means separating the assumptions from the facts.

Personal perspectives and assumptions

Your own preferences, values, and prejudices—which influence your perspective—can affect how accurately you view information. A student who thinks that the death penalty is wrong, for example, may have a hard time analyzing the facts and arguments in an article that supports it. Or, in a research situation, he might use only materials that agree with his perspective.

Consider the perspectives and assumptions that might follow from your values. Then, when you have to analyze information, try to set them aside. "Anticipate your reactions and prejudices and then consciously

resist their influence," says Colby Glass, Professor of Information Research and Philosophy at Palo Alto College.[10]

In addition to helping you analyze accurately, opening yourself to new perspectives will help you build knowledge. The more you know, the more information you have to work with as you move through life and encounter new problems and decisions. Come to school ready to hear and read new ideas, think about their merits, and make informed decisions about what you believe. Says Sternberg, "We need to . . . see issues from a variety of viewpoints and, especially, to see how other people and other cultures view issues and problems facing the world."[11]

Evaluate information

You've gathered and analyzed your information. You have examined its components, its evidence, its validity, its perspective, and any underlying assumptions. Now, based on an examination of evidence and careful analysis, you *evaluate* whether an idea or piece of information is good or bad, important or unimportant, right or wrong. You then set aside what is not useful and use the rest to form an opinion, possible solution, or decision.

For example, you're working on a group presentation on the effects of television watching on young children. You've gathered information that relates to your topic, come up with an idea, and analyzed whether the information supports this idea. Now you evaluate all of the evidence, presenting what's useful in an organized, persuasive way. Another example: In creating a resume, you decide which information to include that will generate the most interest in potential employers and present you in the best light possible.

See Key 4.4 for some questions you can ask to build and use analytical thinking skills.

---

get analytical! ASSESS ANALYTICAL THINKING SKILLS

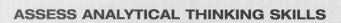

How do you perceive yourself as an analytical thinker? For each statement, circle the number that feels right to you, from 1 for "least like me" to 5 for "most like me."

1. I tend to perform well on objective tests.   ① ② ③ ④ ⑤

2. People say I'm a "thinker," "brainy," "studious."   ① ② ③ ④ ⑤

3. I am not comfortable with gray areas—I prefer information to be laid out in black and white.   ① ② ③ ④ ⑤

4. In a group setting, I like to tackle the details of a problem.   ① ② ③ ④ ⑤

5. I sometimes overthink things and miss my moment of opportunity.   ① ② ③ ④ ⑤

Total your answers here: _____

If your total ranges from 5–12, you consider your analytical thinking skills to be *weak*.

If your total ranges from 13–19, you consider your analytical thinking skills to be *average*.

If your total ranges from 20–25, you consider your analytical thinking skills to be *strong*.

To gather information, ask:	• What requirements does my goal have?
	• What kinds of information do I need to meet my goal?
	• What information is available?
	• Where and when is it available? Where and when can I access it?
	• Of the sources I found, which ones will best help me achieve my goal?

To analyze, ask:	• What are the parts of this information?
	• What is similar to this information? What is different?
	• What are the reasons for this? Why did this happen?
	• What ideas or themes emerge from this material?
	• How would you categorize this information?
	• What conclusions can you make about this information?

To see if examples support an idea, ask:	• What examples, or evidence, support the idea?
	• Does the evidence make sense?
	• Does the evidence support the idea/claim?
	• Is this evidence key information that I need to answer my question?
	• Are there examples that might disprove the idea/claim?

To distinguish fact from opinion, ask:	• Do the words in this information signal fact or opinion? (See Key 4.3)
	• What is the source of this information? Is the source reliable?
	• How does this information compare to other facts or opinions?
	• If this is an opinion, is it supported by facts?
	• How can I use this fact or opinion?

To examine perspectives and assumptions, ask:	• Who is the author? What perspectives might this person have?
	• What might be emphasized or left out as a result of the perspective?
	• How could I consider this information from a different perspective?
	• What assumptions might lie behind this statement or material?
	• How could I prove, or disprove, an assumption?
	• What contradictory assumptions might be equally valid?
	• How might a personal perspective or assumption affect the way I see this material?

To evaluate, ask:	• Do I agree with this information?
	• Does this information fit what I'm trying to prove or accomplish?
	• Is this information true or false, and why?
	• How important is this information?
	• Which ideas or pieces of information would I choose to focus on?

Adapted from www-ed.fnal.gov/trc/tutorial/taxonomy.html (Richard Paul, *Critical Thinking: How to Prepare Students for a Rapidly Changing World,* 1993) and from www.kcmetro.edu/longview/ctac/blooms.htm, Barbara Fowler, Longview Community College "Bloom's Taxonomy and Critical Thinking."

Analytical thinking is only part of the picture. Pursuing your goals, in school and in the workplace, requires not just analyzing information but also thinking creatively about how to use it.

How can you improve your *creative thinking* skills?

Some researchers define creativity as combining existing elements in an innovative way to create a new purpose or result. For example, 3M researcher Spencer Silver, in 1970, created a weak adhesive; four years later, another 3M scientist, Arthur Fry, used it for a hymnal marker. Post-It Notes are now an office staple. Others see creativity as the art of generating ideas from taking a fresh look at how things are related (noting what ladybugs eat inspired organic farmers to bring them in to consume crop-destroying aphids).[12] Still others, including Sternberg, define it as the ability to make unusual connections—to view information in quirky ways that bring about unique results.

To think creatively is to generate new ideas that often go against conventional wisdom and may bring change. Consider how, in the 1940s, mathematician Grace Murray Hopper pioneered the effort to create computer languages that non-mathematicians could understand, and her efforts opened the world of computers to a wide audience.

Creativity is not limited to inventions. For example, Smith College junior Meghan E. Taugher used her creative mind in two ways. First, she

Creativity connects analytical and practical thinking.

key 4.5

and her study group, as part of their class on electrical circuits, devised a solar-powered battery for a laptop computer. "We took the professor's laptop, put all the parts together, and sat outside watching it with a little device to see how much power it was saving. When it fully charged the battery, it was one of those times I felt that what I was learning was true, because I was putting it to use in real life."[13] Second, her experience led her to generate an idea of a new major and career plan—engineering.

Creativity forms a bridge between analytical and practical thinking. You need to think analytically to evaluate the quality of your creative ideas. You also need to think practically to implement them.

Where does creativity come from? Some people, through luck or natural inclination, seem to come up with inspired ideas more often than others. However, creative thinking, like analytical thinking, is a skill that can be developed. Creativity expert Roger von Oech says that mental flexibility is essential. "Like race-car drivers who shift in and out of different gears depending on where they are on the course," he says, you can enhance your creativity by learning to "shift in and out of different types of thinking depending on the needs of the situation at hand."[14]

The following strategies will help you make those shifts and build your ability to think creatively. Note that, because creative ideas often pop up at random, writing them down as they arise will help you remember them. Keep a pen and paper by your bed, your PDA in your pocket, a notepad in your car so that you can grab ideas before they fade from your mind.

Brainstorm

Brainstorming—letting your mind free-associate to come up with different ideas or answers—is also referred to as *divergent thinking:* You start with a question and then let your mind diverge—go in many different directions—in search of solutions. Think of brainstorming as *deliberate* creative thinking—you go into it fully aware that you are attempting to create new ideas. When you brainstorm, generate ideas without thinking about how useful they are; evaluate their quality later. Brainstorming works well in groups because group members can become inspired by, and make creative use of, one another's ideas.[15]

One way to inspire ideas when brainstorming is to think of similar situations—in other words, to make analogies. For example, the discovery of Velcro is a product of analogy: When imagining how two pieces of fabric could stick to each other, the inventor thought of the similar situation of a burr sticking to clothing.

ANALOGY

A comparison based on a resemblance of things otherwise unlike.

When you are brainstorming ideas, don't get hooked on finding the one right answer. Questions may have many "right answers"—or many answers that have degrees of usefulness. The more possibilities you generate, the better your chance of finding the best one. Also, don't stop the process when you think you have the best answer—keep going until you are out of steam. You never know what may come up in those last gasps of creative energy.[16]

Shift your perspective

Just because everyone believes something doesn't make it so; just because something "has always been that way" doesn't make it good. Changing how you look at a situation or problem can inspire creative ideas. Here are some ways to do it:

Challenge assumptions. In the late 1960s, conventional wisdom said that school provided education and television provided entertainment. Jim Henson, a pioneer in children's television, asked, "Why can't we use TV to educate young children?" From that question, the characters of *Sesame Street*—and a host of other educational programs—were born.

It is better to have enough ideas for some of them to be wrong, than to be always right by having no ideas at all.

EDWARD DE BONO

Take a new and different look. Try on new perspectives by asking others for their views, reading about new ways to approach situations, or deliberately going with the opposite of your first instinct.[17] Then use those perspectives to inspire creativity. For your English Lit course, analyze a novel from the point of view of one of the main characters. For Political Science, craft a position paper for a presidential or senatorial candidate. Perception puzzles are a fun way to experience how looking at something in a new way can bring a totally different idea (see Key 4.6).

Ask "what if" questions. Set up hypothetical environments in which new ideas can grow: "What if I knew I couldn't fail?" "What if I had unlimited money or time?" Ideas will emerge from your "what if" questions. For example, the founders of Seeds of Peace, faced with generations of conflict in the Middle East, asked: What if Israeli and Palestinian teens met at a summer camp in Maine so that the next generation has greater under-

Try these perception puzzles.

key
4.6

is this a face or a musician?

lines or a letter?

a duck or a bunny?

Face puzzle: Roger Shepard, *Mind Sights.* Henry Holt & Company.

standing and respect than the last? And what if follow-up programs and reunions are set up to cement friendships so that relationships change the politics of the Middle East? Based on the ideas that came up, they created an organization to prepare teenagers from the Middle East with the leadership skills needed to coexist peacefully.

Set the stage for creativity

Use these strategies to give yourself the best possible chance at generating creative ideas.

Choose—or create—environments that free your mind. Find places that energize you. Play music that moves you. Paint your study walls your favorite color. Seek out people who inspire you. Sternberg agrees: "Find the environment that rewards what you have to offer," he says, "and then make the most of your creativity and of yourself in that environment."[18]

Be curious. Try something you consider new and different—take a course that is completely unlike your major, try a new sport or game, listen to a new genre of music, read a magazine or book that you've never seen before. Seeking out new experiences and ideas will broaden your knowledge, giving you more raw material with which to build creative ideas.[19]

Give yourself time to "sit" with a question. American society values speed, so much so that to say someone is "quick" is to consider that person intelligent.[20] Equating speed with intelligence can stifle creativity, because many creative ideas come when you allow time for thoughts to percolate. Take breaks when figuring out a problem. Take the pressure off by getting some exercise, napping, talking with a friend, working on something else, doing something fun. Creative ideas often come when you give your brain permission to "leave the job" for a while.[21]

Believe in yourself as a creative thinker. While it is normal to want critical approval and success for your creative efforts, you may not get it right away, especially if your ideas break new ground. When Gustav Mahler's Symphony No. 2—the Resurrection Symphony—was performed in 1910, critics walked out of the concert hall because of its innovative sound. Today, the Resurrection Symphony is considered one of the formative compositions of this era. Like Mahler, you must believe in your creative expression, no matter what others say. Critics, after all, can be wrong or simply a step or two behind.

Take risks

Creative breakthroughs can come from sensible risk-taking.

Fly in the face of convention. Entrepreneur Michael Dell turned tradition on its ear when he took a "tell me what you want and I will build it for you" approach to computer marketing instead of a "build it and they will buy it" approach. The possibility of failure did not stop him from risking money, time, energy, and reputation to achieve a truly unique and creative goal.

Let mistakes be okay. Open yourself to the learning that comes from not being afraid to mess up. Sternberg reports that ". . . in the course of their schooling . . . children learn that it's not all right to make mistakes. As a result, they become afraid to err and thus to risk the kind of independent, if sometimes flawed, thinking" that can promote creative ideas.[22] When Dr. Hunter—successful inventor of the drug-coated coronary stent—and his company failed to develop a particular treatment for multiple sclerosis, he said, "You have to celebrate the failures. If you send the message that the only road to career success is experiments that work, people won't ask risky questions, or get any dramatically new answers."[23]

As with analytical thinking, asking questions powers creative thinking. See Key 4.7 for examples of the kinds of questions you can ask to get your creative juices flowing.

When you are working to solve a problem or decision, creative thinking allows you to generate possible solutions and choices. However, choices aren't enough and potential solutions must be tried out. You need practical thinking in order to make the best solution or choice happen.

Ask these questions to jump-start creative thinking.

To brainstorm, ask:	● What do I want to accomplish?
	● What are the craziest ideas I can think of?
	● What are ten ways that I can reach my goal?
	● What ideas or strategies have worked before and how can I apply them?
	● How else can this be done?
To shift your perspective, ask:	● How has this always been done—and what would be a different way?
	● What is another way to look at this situation?
	● How can I approach this task from a completely new angle?
	● How would others do this? How would they view this?
	● What if. . . ?
To set the stage for creativity, ask:	● Where and with whom do I feel relaxed and inspired?
	● What music helps me think out of the box?
	● When in the day or night am I most likely to experience a flow of creative ideas?
	● What do I think would be new and interesting to try, to see, to read?
	● What is the most outrageous outcome of a situation that I can imagine?
To take risks, ask:	● What is the conventional way of doing this? What would be a totally different way?
	● What would be a risky approach to this problem or question?
	● What choice would people caution me about and why?
	● What is the worst that can happen if I take this risk? What is the best?
	● What have I learned from this mistake?

ASSESS CREATIVE THINKING SKILLS

How do you perceive yourself as a creative thinker? For each statement, circle the number that feels right to you, from 1 for "least like me" to 5 for "most like me."

1. I tend to resist rules and regulations.   ① ② ③ ④ ⑤
2. People say I'm "expressive," "full of ideas," "innovative."   ① ② ③ ④ ⑤
3. I break out of my routine and find new experiences.   ① ② ③ ④ ⑤
4. In a group setting, I like to toss ideas into the ring.   ① ② ③ ④ ⑤
5. If you say something is too risky, I'm all for it.   ① ② ③ ④ ⑤

Total your answers here: _____

If your total ranges from 5–12, you consider your creative thinking skills to be *weak*.

If your total ranges from 13–19, you consider your creative thinking skills to be *average*.

If your total ranges from 20–25, you consider your creative thinking skills to be *strong*.

How can you improve your *practical thinking* skills?

Practical thinking—also called "common sense" or "street smarts"— refers to how you adapt to your environment, or shape or change your environment to adapt to you, in order to pursue important goals. A basic example: Your goal is to pass your required freshman composition course. You are a visual learner in a verbally-focused classroom. To achieve your goal, you can build your verbal skills (adapt to your environment) or ask the instructor and your study group to help you present information in visual terms (change your environment to adapt to you)—or both.

Why do you need to think practically? Since many academic problems can be solved with analytical thinking alone, it's easy to get the impression that strong analytical thinking skills translate into life success. However, real-world problems are different than many academic problems—they are often less clear, related closely to your life and needs, and answerable in more than one way. Plus, stakes are often higher—in other words, the way you solve a financial dilemma has a more significant impact on your life than how you work through a geometry proof. Successfully solving real-world problems demands a practical approach.[24]

Practical thinking allows you to bridge the gap between what makes a successful student and what brings real-world success. In other words, even if you ace the courses for your math and education double major, you also need to be able to apply what you learned in a specific job.

The accomplishments of David Hosei, a student at Indiana University, show how practical thinking makes things happen. As a finance and entrepreneurship major, Hosei has built extensive knowledge in business and money matters. Pursuing a goal to help others, Hosei formed HELP

(Help Educate Lots of People), a nonprofit organization, to teach peers about money management. In addition, he organizes an annual fundraiser—the IU Battle of the Bands—to raise money for Jill's House, a refuge for families seeking cancer treatments at a local medical center.[25]

Experience helps develop practical thinking skills

You gain much of your ability to think practically—your common sense—from personal experience, rather than from formal lessons. This knowledge is an important tool in achieving goals.[26]

What you learn from experience answers "how" questions—how to talk, how to behave, how to proceed.[27] For example, after completing a few papers for a particular course, you may pick up cues about how to impress that instructor. Following a couple of conflicts with a partner, you may learn how to avoid sore spots when the conversation heats up. See Key 4.8 for ways in which this kind of knowledge can be shown in "if-then" statements.

There are two keys to making practical knowledge work for you. First, make an active choice to learn from experience—to pay attention to how things work at school, in personal relationships, and at work. Second, make sure you apply what you learn, assuring that you will not have

One way to map out what you learn from experience.

key 4.8

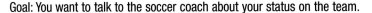

Goal: You want to talk to the soccer coach about your status on the team.

IF the team has had a good practice and IF you've played well during the scrimmage and IF the coach isn't rushing off somewhere, THEN grab a moment with him right after practice ends.

IF the team is having a tough time and IF you've been sidelined and IF the coach is in a rush and stressed, THEN drop in on his office hours tomorrow.

to learn the same lessons over and over again. As Sternberg says, "what matters most is not how much experience you have had but rather how much you have profited from it—in other words, how well you apply what you have learned."[28]

The emotional intelligence connection

Part of what you learn from experience involves *emotional intelligence*. Based on the work of psychologist Daniel Goleman, your emotional intelligence quotient (EQ) is the set of personal and social competencies that involve knowing yourself, mastering your feelings, and developing social skills.[29] *Social competence*—involving skills such as sensing other people's feelings and needs, getting your message across to others, managing conflict, leading and bonding with people—usually is built through experience rather than by reading theory or a how-to manual.

Emotional intelligence has a significant effect on your ability to communicate and maneuver in a social environment in a way that helps you achieve your goals. It will be examined in greater detail in the section on communication in Chapter 9.

Practical thinking means action

Learning different ways to take action and stay in motion builds your practical thinking ability. Strategies you learn throughout this course will keep you moving toward your goals30:

- Stay motivated. Use techniques from Chapter 1 to persevere when you face a problem. Get started on achieving results instead of dwelling on exactly how to start. Translate thoughts into concrete actions instead of getting bogged down in "analysis paralysis."

- Make the most of your personal strengths. What you've learned in Chapter 2 will help you see what you do best—and use those strengths as you apply practical solutions.

- When things go wrong, accept responsibility and reject self-pity. You know from Chapter 1 that failure is an excellent teacher. Learn from what happened, act on what you have learned, and don't let self-pity stall your momentum.

- Focus on the goal and avoid distractions. Keep your eye on the big picture and complete what you've planned, rather than getting lost in the details. Don't let personal problems or other distractions take you off the track.

- Manage time and tasks effectively. Use what you know from Chapter 2 to plan your time in a way that promotes goal accomplishment. Avoid the pitfalls of procrastination. Accurately gauge what you can handle—don't take on too many projects, or too few

- Believe in yourself. Have faith in your ability to achieve what you set out to do.

See Key 4.9 for some questions you can ask in order to apply practical thinking to your problems and decisions.

To learn from experience, ask:	• What worked well, or not so well, about my approach? My timing? My tone? My wording?
	• What did others like or not like about what I did?
	• What did I learn from that experience, conversation, event?
	• How would I change things if I had to do it over again?
	• What do I know I would do again?

To apply what you learn, ask:	• What have I learned that would work here?
	• What have I seen others do, or heard about from them, that would be helpful here?
	• What does this situation have in common with past situations I've been involved in?
	• What has worked in similar situations in the past?

To boost your ability to take action, ask:	• How can I get motivated and remove limitations?
	• How can I, in this situation, make the most of what I do well?
	• If I fail, what can I learn from it?
	• What steps will get me to my goal, and what trade-offs are involved?
	• How can I manage my time more effectively?

get practical!

ASSESS PRACTICAL THINKING SKILLS

How do you perceive yourself as a practical thinker? For each statement, circle the number that feels right to you, from 1 for "least like me" to 5 for "most like me."

1. I can find a way around any obstacle. ① ② ③ ④ ⑤
2. People say I'm a "doer," the "go-to" person, "organized." ① ② ③ ④ ⑤
3. When I have a vision, I translate it into steps from A to B to C. ① ② ③ ④ ⑤
4. In a group setting, I like to set up the plan. ① ② ③ ④ ⑤
5. I don't like to leave loose ends dangling—I'm a finisher. ① ② ③ ④ ⑤

Total your answers here: _____

If your total ranges from 5–12, you consider your practical thinking skills to be *weak*.

If your total ranges from 13–19, you consider your practical thinking skills to be *average*.

If your total ranges from 20–25, you consider your practical thinking skills to be *strong*.

Your skills at a glance: In the sections of the triangle, write your assessment scores from *Get Analytical (p. 12)*, *Get Creative (p. 19)*, and *Get Practical (above)*. Looking at the scores together will give you an idea of how you perceive your skills in all three aspects of successful intelligence, and will help you think about where you may want to build strength.

PROBLEM SOLVING	THINKING SKILL	DECISION MAKING
Define the problem—recognize that something needs to change, identify what's happening, look for true causes	**STEP 1** DEFINE	Define the decision—identify your goal (your need) and then construct a decision that will help you get it
Analyze the problem—gather information, break it down into pieces, verify facts, look at perspectives and assumptions, evaluate information	**STEP 2** ANALYZE	Examine needs and motives—consider the layers of needs carefully, and be honest about what you really want
Generate possible solutions—use creative strategies to think of ways you could address the causes of this problem	**STEP 3** CREATE	Name and/or generate different options—use creative questions to come up with choices that would fulfill your needs
Evaluate solutions—look carefully at potential pros and cons of each, and choose what seems best	**STEP 4** ANALYZE (EVALUATE)	Evaluate options—look carefully at potential pros and cons of each, and choose what seems best
Put the solution to work—persevere, focus on results, and believe in yourself as you go for your goal	**STEP 5** TAKE PRACTICAL ACTION	Act on your decision—go down the path and use practical strategies to stay on target
Evaluate how well the solution worked—look at the effects of what you did	**STEP 6** ANALYZE (RE-EVALUATE)	Evaluate the success of your decision—look at whether it accomplished what you had hoped
In the future, apply what you've learned—use this solution, or a better one, when a similar situation comes up again	**STEP 7** TAKE PRACTICAL ACTION	In the future, apply what you've learned—make this choice, or a better one, when a similar decision comes up again

How can you put *analytical, creative, and practical thinking together* to solve a problem or make a decision?

You have developed your understanding of what it means to think analytically, creatively, and practically. You have explored your perception of where your strengths and weaknesses lie. Now you will see how to put analytical, creative, and practical thinking together to solve problems and make decisions successfully—at school, in the workplace, or in your personal life.

Problem solving and decision making follow similar paths. Both require you to identify and analyze a situation, generate possibilities, choose one, follow through on it, and evaluate its success. Key 4.10 gives an overview of the paths, indicating how you think at each step.

How do you choose which path to follow? Understanding the differences will help. First of all, problem solving generally requires more focus on coming up with possible solutions; when you face a decision, your

SITUATION	YOU HAVE A PROBLEM IF . . .	YOU NEED TO MAKE A DECISION IF . . .
Planning summer activities	Your low GPA means you need to attend summer school—and you've already accepted a summer job.	You've been accepted into two summer abroad internship programs.
Declaring a major	It's time to declare but you don't have all the prerequisites for the major you want.	There are three majors that appeal to you and you qualify for them all.
Relationships with instructors	You are having trouble following the lecture style of a particular instructor.	Your psychology survey course has seven sections taught by different instructors; you have to choose one.

choices are often determined. Second, problem solving aims to remove or counteract negative effects; decision making aims to fulfill a need. See Key 4.11 for some examples. Remember, too, that whereas all problem solving requires you to make a decision—when you decide on a solution—only some decision making requires you to solve a problem.

Solving a problem

A problem exists when a situation has negative effects. Recognizing that there is a problem—being aware of those effects—is essential before you can begin to solve it. In other words, your first move is to go from the effects—"I'm unhappy/uneasy/angry"—to determining why: "My schedule is overwhelming me." "I'm over my head in this course." "My credit card debt is out of control." Then you begin the problem-solving process in earnest.

What happens if you *don't* act in a successfully intelligent way? Take, for example, a student having an issue with an instructor. He may get into an argument with the instructor during class time. He may stop showing up to class. He may not make an effort with assignments. All of these choices will most likely have bad consequences for him.

Now look at how this student might work through this problem using his analytical, creative, and practical thinking skills. Key 4.12 shows how his effort can pay off.

As you go through the problem-solving process, keep these tips in mind.

Use probing questions to define problems. Focus on causes. If you are not happy in a class, for example, you could ask questions like these:

● What do I think about when I feel unhappy?

● Do my feelings involve my instructor? My classmates?

● Is the subject matter difficult? The volume of work too much?

Chances are that how you answer one or more of these questions may lead to a clear definition—and ultimately to the right solution.

Working through a problem relating to an instructor.

DEFINE PROBLEM HERE:	ANALYZE THE PROBLEM
I don't like my Freshman Composition instructor	We have different views and personality types— I don't feel respected or heard. I'm not interested in being there and my grades are suffering from my lack of motivation.

Use boxes below to list possible solutions:

POTENTIAL POSITIVE EFFECTS	SOLUTION #1	POTENTIAL NEGATIVE EFFECTS
List for each solution: Don't have to deal with that instructor Less stress	Drop the course	*List for each solution:* Grade gets entered on my transcript I'll have to take the course eventually; it's required for my major

POTENTIAL POSITIVE EFFECTS	SOLUTION #2	POTENTIAL NEGATIVE EFFECTS
Getting credit for the course Feeling like I've honored a commitment	Put up with it until the end of the semester	Stress every time I'm there Lowered motivation Probably not such a good final grade

POTENTIAL POSITIVE EFFECTS	SOLUTION #3	POTENTIAL NEGATIVE EFFECTS
A chance to express myself Could get good advice An opportunity to ask direct questions of the instructor	Schedule meetings with advisor and instructor	Have to face instructor one-on-one Might just make things worse

Now choose the solution you think is best—circle it and make it happen.

ACTUAL POSITIVE EFFECTS	PRACTICAL ACTION	ACTUAL NEGATIVE EFFECTS
List for chosen solution: Got some helpful advice from advisor Talking in person with the instructor actually promoted a fairly honest discussion I won't have to take the course again	I scheduled and attended meetings with both advisor and instructor, and opted to stick with the course.	*List for chosen solution:* The discussion was difficult and sometimes tense I still don't know how much learning I'll retain from this course

FINAL EVALUATION: Was it a good or bad solution?

The solution has improved things. I'll finish the course, and even though the instructor and I aren't the best of friends, we have a mutual understanding now. I feel more respected and more willing to put my time into the course.

Analyze carefully. Gather all the information you can, so that you can consider the situation comprehensively. Consider what you can learn from how the problem is similar to, or different from, other problems. Clarify facts. Note your own perspective, and ask others for theirs. Make sure you are not looking at the problem through the lens of an assumption.

No problem can stand the assault of sustained thinking.

VOLTAIRE

Generate possible solutions based on causes, not effects. Addressing a cause provides a lasting solution, whereas "fixing" an effect cannot. Say your shoulder hurts when you use your computer. Getting a friend to massage it is a nice but temporary solution, because the pain returns whenever you go back to work. Changing the height of your keyboard and mouse is a better idea, because it eliminates the cause of your pain.

Making a decision

Psychologists who have studied decision making have learned that many random factors influence the choices people make. For example, you may choose a major, not because you love the subject, but because you think your parents will approve of it. The goal is to make well-considered decisions despite factors that may derail your thinking.

What happens when you make important decisions quickly, without using your analytical, creative, and practical thinking skills? Consider a student trying to decide whether to transfer schools. If she stays at her current school because a good friend says, "You can't leave me!" or transfers because she doesn't like her living situation, she may question her choice later—most likely because she didn't consider cause and effect carefully when deciding.

Now look at how this student might make a successfully intelligent decision. Key 4.13 shows how she worked through the analytical, creative, and practical parts of the process.

As you use the steps in Key 4.13 to make a decision, remember these hints.

Look at the given options—then try to think of more. Some decisions have a given set of options. For example, your school may allow you to major, double major, or major and minor. However, when you are making your decision, you may be able to brainstorm with an advisor to come up with more options—such as an interdisciplinary major you create on your own.

Think about how your decision affects others. For example, the student thinking about a transfer considers the impact on friends and family. What she concludes about that impact may inform when she transfers and even the school she chooses.

Making a decision about whether to transfer schools.

DEFINE THE DECISION	EXAMINE NEEDS AND MOTIVES
Whether or not to transfer schools	I attend a small private college. My father has changed jobs and can no longer afford my tuition. My goal is to become a physical therapist, so I need a school with a full physical therapy program. My family needs to cut costs. I need to transfer credits.

Use boxes below to list possible choices:

POTENTIAL POSITIVE EFFECTS	CHOICE #1	POTENTIAL NEGATIVE EFFECTS
List for each solution:	Continue at the current college	*List for each solution:*
No need to adjust to a new place or new people		Need to finance most of my tuition and costs on my own
Ability to continue course work as planned		Difficult to find time for a job
		Might not qualify for aid

	CHOICE #2	
Opportunity to connect with some high school friends	Transfer to a state college	Need to earn some money or get financial aid
Cheaper tuition and room costs		Physical therapy program is small and not very strong
Credits will transfer		

	CHOICE #3	
Many physical therapy courses available	Transfer to the community college	No personal contacts there that I know of
School is close so I could live at home and save room costs		Less independence if I live at home
Reasonable tuition; credits will transfer		No bachelor's degree available

Now choose the one you think is best—circle it and make it happen.

ACTUAL POSITIVE EFFECTS	PRACTICAL ACTION	ACTUAL NEGATIVE EFFECTS
List for chosen solution:	Go to community college for two years; then transfer to a four-year school to get a B.A. and complete physical therapy course work.	*List for chosen solution:*
Money saved,		Loss of some independence
Opportunity to spend time on studies rather than on working to earn tuition money		Less contact with friends
Availability of classes I need		

FINAL EVALUATION: Was it a good or bad choice?

I'm satisfied with the decision. It can be hard being at home at times, but my parents are adjusting to my independence and I'm trying to respect their concerns. With fewer social distractions, I'm really getting my work done. Plus the financial aspect of the decision is ideal.

Critical, Creative, and Practical Thinking **27**

Gather perspectives. Talk with others who have made similar decisions. There are more ways of doing things than one brain can possibly imagine on its own.

Look at the long-term effects. For important decisions, do a short-term evaluation and another evaluation after a period of time. See whether your decision has sent you down a path that has continued to bring positive effects.

Keeping your balance

No one has equal strengths in analytical, creative, and practical thinking. Adjusting your expectations to match what you can accomplish is a key principle of successful intelligence. It requires that you:

- use what you've learned in this chapter and the rest of the text to maximize your analytical, creative, and practical abilities
- reflect on what you do well, and focus on strengthening weaker skills
- combine all three thinking skills to accomplish your goals, knowing when and how to apply your analytical, creative, and practical abilities
- believe in your skills as a thinker

"Successfully intelligent people," says Sternberg, "defy negative expectations, even when these expectations arise from low scores on IQ or similar tests. They do not let other people's assessments stop them from achieving their goals. They find their path and then pursue it, realizing that there will be obstacles along the way and that surmounting these obstacles is part of the challenge."[31] Let the obstacles come, as they will for everyone, in all aspects of life. You can face and overcome them with the power of your successfully intelligent thinking.

Κρινειν

The word "critical" is derived from the Greek word *krinein*, which means to separate in order to choose or select. Successful intelligence requires that you separate, evaluate, and select ideas and information as you think through problematic situations. Says Sternberg, "It is more important to know when and how to use these aspects of successful intelligence than just to have them."[32]

Think of this concept as you use your analytical, creative, and practical thinking skills to solve problems, make decisions, innovate, and question. Consider information carefully, and separate out and select the best approaches. Successful intelligence gives you the power to choose how to respond to information, people, and events in ways that help you reach your goals.

PERSONAL TRIUMPH

SUSIE IVY, Fashion Design major; Dominican University, River Forest, Illinois

Discovering personal power can turn a life around. As mentors and activities helped Susie Ivy deal with her past and learn of her strength and creativity, she found ways to achieve that she never would have imagined.

People tell me I'm motivated and that I take initiative to make good things happen. It's funny because I see myself as a pretty laid-back person. But I do believe having someone who believes in you can make a difference. Everyone needs to be lifted up, at least once in a while.

I am the youngest of five children. My mother suffered from schizophrenia, and she was addicted to drugs. When my aunt called the Department of Child and Family Services and reported our situation, my brothers and sisters and I were placed in foster care. I was five years old.

We all were placed in the same home, where at times there were as many as 10 foster children living. Although we weren't physically abused, we didn't get the emotional support we needed. We didn't receive counseling, and no one ever explained how long we would be in foster care or what to expect. For years I fantasized that our mother would get her life together and bring us home. But that never happened.

When I was eight years old, we started attending a church youth group. I really enjoyed the activities and the youth leaders. I participated in the weekly meetings and went to summer camp. One of the youth leaders is still my mentor today. As I think back, I realize that this is when my positive childhood memories began to form.

During my teen years, many girls at my high school got pregnant and left school. Although I wasn't happy at home, I knew I didn't want that to be my fate. Instead, I joined the track and swim teams. I swam all four years and won most valuable player each year. Discovering something I was good at had a profound impact on the way I saw myself. I set out to prove that I was smart and talented.

Before graduation, I made plans to attend college, thinking I wanted to be a surgical nurse. In my senior year, I changed my mind. I was talking with a few friends about the prom and decided to make my own dress. I couldn't draw well, so I described the dress to my foster dad, and he drew it for me. I was so pleased with how the dress turned out! Right then and there I decided to major in fashion design, and I began applying to colleges that offered fashion design programs.

I love my major. I like exploring the creative process and pushing myself to do my best. Every year, my school sponsors a spring fashion show, and my clothes are modeled in front of an audience. Last year, I was selected from my school to go to New York City for a fashion tour, where I saw new designs and visited other colleges. These are the highlights of my college experience.

I've also discovered that competition is a motivating force in my life, especially when it comes to my designs. For example, a girl in one of my classes comes from a rich family. She can afford the nicest fabrics for her projects, and she doesn't have to work like I do to pay for school. But I remind myself that money can't buy talent. Everybody who is famous didn't start with a lot of money. When I think about where I've been, I'm happy about who I'm becoming.

29

BUILDING SKILLS

FOR COLLEGE, CAREER, AND LIFE SUCCESS

Developing Successful Intelligence

PUTTING IT ALL TOGETHER

Make an important decision. Put the decision-making process to work on something that matters to you. You will apply your analytical, creative, and practical thinking skills. Use a separate sheet of paper for steps 2 and 3.

Step 1. *Analyze: Define the decision.* Write an important long-term goal that you have, and define the decision that will help you fulfill it. Example: "My goal is to become a nurse. My decision: What to specialize in."

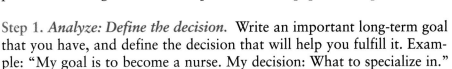

Step 2. *Analyze: Examine needs and concerns.* What do you want? What are your needs, and how do your values come into play? What needs of others will you need to take into account? What roadblocks might be involved? List everything you come up with. For example, the prospective nurse might list needs like: "I need to feel that I'm helping people. I intend to help with the nursing shortage. I need to make a good living."

Step 3. *Be creative: Generate options.* Ask questions to imagine what's possible. Where might you work? What might be the schedule and pace? Who might work with you? What would you see, smell, and hear on your job? What would you do every day? List, too, all of the options you know of. The prospective nurse, for example, might list ER, pediatrics, surgery, oncology, geriatrics, and so on. Brainstorm other options that might not seem so obvious.

create your future

Step 4. *Analyze: Evaluate options.* Think about how well your options will fulfill your needs. For two of your options, write potential positive and negative effects (pros and cons) of each.

Option 1: _____

Potential pros: _____

_____

Potential cons: _____

_____

Option 2: _____

Potential pros: _____

_____

Potential cons: _____

_____

Step 5. *Get Practical: Imagine acting on your decision.* Describe one practical course of action, based on your thinking so far, that you might follow. List the specific steps you would take. For example, the prospective nurse might list actions that help him determine what type of nursing suits him best, such as interning, summer jobs, academic goals, and talking to working nurses.

_____

_____

_____

Finally, over time, plan to put your decision into action. Eventually you will need to complete the two final steps of the process. Step 6 is to evaluate the decision: How did it work out? Analyze whether you, and others, got what you needed. Step 7 is to practically apply what you've learned from the decision to other decisions you make in the future.

Team Building

COLLABORATIVE SOLUTIONS

Powerful group problem solving. On a 3x5 card or a plain sheet of paper, each student in the class writes a school-related problem—this could be a fear, a challenge, a sticky situation, or a roadblock. Students hand these in without names. The instructor writes the list up on the board.

Divide into groups of two to four. Each group chooses one problem to work on (try not to have two groups working on the same problem). Use the empty problem-solving flowchart on p. 34 to fill in your work.

1. *Analyze: Define the problem.* As a group, look at the negative effects and state your problem specifically. Then, explore and write down the causes.

2. *Analyze: Examine the problem.* Pick it apart to see what's happening. Gather information from all group members, verify facts, go beyond assumptions.

3. *Create: Generate possible solutions.* From the most likely causes of the problem, derive possible solutions. Record all the ideas that group members offer. After 10 minutes or so, each group member should choose one possible solution to evaluate independently.

4. *Analyze: Evaluate each solution.* In thinking independently through the assigned solution, each group member should (a) weigh the positive and negative effects, (b) consider similar problems, and (c) describe how the solution affects the causes of the problem. Evaluate your assigned solution. Is it a good one? Will it work?

5. *Get Practical: Choose a solution.* Group members then come together, share observations and recommendations, and then take a vote: Which solution is the best? You may have a tie or may want to combine two different solutions. Try to find the solution that works for most of the group. Then, together, come up with a plan for how you would put your solution to work.

6. *Analyze: Evaluate your solution.* As a group, share and discuss what you had individually imagined the positive and negative effects of this solution would be. Try to come to an agreement on how you think the solution would work out.

Writing

DISCOVERY THROUGH JOURNALING

Record your thoughts on a separate piece of paper or in a journal.

Wiser choices. Think about a choice you made that, looking back, you wish you had handled differently. First, describe what the decision was, what option you chose, and what the consequences were. Then, write about what you would do if you could make the decision again. What did you learn from your experience that you can apply to other decisions? How could being analytical, creative, and practical have helped you reach a more effective outcome?

Career Portfolio

PLAN FOR SUCCESS

Generating ideas for internships. People often put more time and effort into deciding what cell phone to buy than they do with life-altering decisions like how to prepare for career success. Pursuing internships is part of a comprehensive career decision-making process. It's a practical

Work through a problem using this flow chart.

DEFINE PROBLEM HERE: ANALYZE THE PROBLEM

Use boxes below to list possible solutions:

POTENTIAL POSITIVE EFFECTS	SOLUTION #1	POTENTIAL NEGATIVE EFFECTS
List for each solution:		*List for each solution:*

SOLUTION #2

SOLUTION #3

Now choose the solution you think is best—circle it and make it happen.

ACTUAL POSITIVE EFFECTS	PRACTICAL ACTION	ACTUAL NEGATIVE EFFECTS
List for chosen solution:		*List for chosen solution:*

FINAL EVALUATION: Was it a good or bad solution?

way to get experience, learn what you like and don't like, and make valuable connections.

Fill in the following:

Career areas that I'm considering. Why?

1. _____ *Because:* _____

2. _____ *Because:* _____

3. _____ *Because:* _____

People who I want to interview about their fields/professions. Why?

1. _____ *Because:* _____

2. _____ *Because:* _____

3. _____ *Because:* _____

Next, take practical steps to investigate internships. Talk to the people you listed. Contact companies you would like to work for and see what internship opportunities are available. Talk with someone in your school's career office. If a company doesn't offer internships, ask them if you might be the pioneer intern.

Finally, after you have gathered some useful information, use a separate sheet of paper to creatively envision your internship experience. Describe it: What would it look like? What would you do each day? Each week? Where would you go? With whom would you work? What would you contribute with your gifts and talents? Make it happen with your successful intelligence.

SUGGESTED READINGS

Cameron, Julia with Mark Bryan. *The Artist's Way: A Spiritual Path to Higher Creativity*. New York: G.P. Putnam's Sons, 1995.

deBono, Edward. *Lateral Thinking: Creativity Step by Step*. New York: Perennial Library, 1990.

Goleman, Daniel. *Emotional Intelligence: Why It Can Matter More Than IQ*. New York: Bantam, 1995.

Moscovich, Ivan. *1000 Playthinks*. New York: Workman Publishing, 2001.

Noone, Donald J., Ph.D. *Creative Problem Solving*. New York: Barron's, 1998.

Sark. Living Juicy: *Daily Morsels for Your Creative Soul*. Berkeley, CA: Celestial Arts, 1994.

von Oech, Roger. *A Kick in the Seat of the Pants*. New York: Harper & Row Publishers, 1986.

von Oech, Roger. *A Whack on the Side of the Head*. New York: Warner Books, 1998.

INTERNET RESOURCES

Creativity at Work (resources for workplace creativity): www.creativityatwork.com

Creativity for Life (tips and strategies for creativity): www.creativityforlife.com

Roger von Oech's Creative Think Web site: www.creative-think.com

1. Robert J. Sternberg, *Successful Intelligence*. New York: Plume, 1997, p. 12.

2. Ibid, p. 127.

3. Matt Thomas, "What is Higher-Order Thinking and Critical/Creative/Constructive Thinking?" The Center for Studies in Higher-Order Literacy [on-line]. Available: http://members.aol.com/MattT10574/Higher OrderLiteracy.htm#What (April 2004).

4. Sternberg, p. 128.

5. Vincent Ruggiero, *The Art of Thinking*, 2001, quoted in "Critical Thinking," Oregon State University [online]. Available: http://success.oregonstate.edu/study/learning.cfm (April 2004).

6. Richard Paul, "The Role of Questions in Thinking, Teaching, and Learning," The Center for Thinking and Learning, 1995 [on-line]. Available: http://www.criticalthinking.org/University/univclass/roleofquest.html (April 2004).

7. "The Best Innovations Are Those That Come From Smart Questions," *Wall Street Journal*, April 12, 2004, B1.

8. Lawrence F. Lowery, "The Biological Basis of Thinking and Learning," 1998, Full Option Science System at the University of California at Berkeley [on-line]. Available: http://lhsfoss.org/newsletters/archive/pdfs/FOSS_BBTL.pdf (April 2004).

9. Ivan Moscovich, *1000 Playthinks*. New York: Workman Publishing, p. 7.

10. Colby Glass, "Strategies for Critical Thinking," March 1999 [on-line]. Available: http://www.accd.edu/pac/philosop/phil1301/ctstrategies.htm (April 2004).

11. Sternberg, p. 49.

12. Charles Cave (August 1999). "Definitions of Creativity" [on-line]. Available: http://members. ozemail. com.au/~caveman/Creative/Basics/definitions.htm (April 2003).

13. Elizabeth F. Farrell, "Engineering a Warmer Welcome for Female Students: The Discipline Tries to Stress its Social Relevance, an Important Factor for Many Women," *The Chronicle of Higher Education*, February 22, 2002 [on-line]. Available: http://chronicle.com/weekly/v48/ i24/24a03101.htm (March 2004).

14. Roger von Oech, *A Kick in the Seat of the Pants*. New York: Harper & Row Publishers, 1986, pp. 5–21.

15. Dennis Coon, *Introduction to Psychology: Exploration and Application*, 6th ed. St. Paul: West Publishing Company, 1992, p. 295.

16. Roger von Oech, *A Whack on the Side of the Head*. New York: Warner Books, 1990, pp. 11–168.

17. J. R. Hayes, *Cognitive Psychology: Thinking and Creating*. Homewood, IL: Dorsey, 1978.

18. Sternberg, p. 219.

19. Adapted from T. Z. Tardif and R. J. Sternberg, "What Do We Know About Creativity?" in *The Nature of Creativity*, ed. R. J. Sternberg, 1988. London: Cambridge University Press.

20. Sternberg, p. 212.

21. Hayes.

22. Sternberg, p. 202.

23. "The Best Innovations Are Those That Come From Smart Questions," *Wall Street Journal*, April 12, 2004, B1.

24. Sternberg, p. 229–230.

25. "Amazing Student, David Hosei—Entrepreneur with a Heart," Indiana University Web Site, 2003 [online]. Available: http://excellence.indiana.edu/hosei/ (March 2004).

26. Sternberg, p. 236.

27. Robert J. Sternberg and Elena L. Grigorenko, "Practical Intelligence and the Principal," Yale University: Publication Series No. 2, 2001, p. 5.

28. Sternberg, p. 241.

29. Daniel Goleman, *Emotional Intelligence: Why It Can Matter More Than IQ*. (New York: Bantam, 1995).

30. Sternberg, pp. 251–269.

31. Sternberg, p. 19.

32. Sternberg, p. 128.

BECOMING A BETTER TEST TAKER

Because some instructors may schedule exams early and often in the semester, begin right away to develop strategies for test success. Starting off on the right foot will boost your confidence and motivate you to work even harder. The saying that "success breeds more success" couldn't be more true as you begin college.

The material in this Study Break is designed to help you organize yourself as you prepare for exams. As you learn to create a pre-test study plan and schedule, you will also build your ability to use your time efficiently.

When you reach Chapter 7, "Test Taking: Showing What You Know," you will study test taking in depth, including test preparation, test anxiety, general test taking strategies, strategies for handling different types of test questions, and learning from test mistakes.

Decide on a Study Plan

Start your test preparation by deciding what you will study. Go through your notes, texts, related primary sources, and handouts, and set aside materials you don't need. Then prioritize the remaining materials. Your goal is to focus on information that is most likely to be on the exam. Use the test preparation tips in Chapter 7 and the material on studying your text in Chapter 5 to boost your effectiveness as you prepare.

Create a Study Schedule and Checklist

Next, use the time-management and goal-setting skills from Chapter 2 to prepare a schedule. Consider all of the relevant factors—your study materials, the number of days until the test, and the time you can study each day. If you establish your schedule ahead of time and write it in a planner, you are more likely to follow it.

Let our advance worrying become advance thinking and planning.

WINSTON CHURCHILL

Prepare for a Test

A checklist like the one on the following page will help you organize and stay on track as you prepare. Use the checklist for each exam to define your study goals, get organized, and stay on track. Also use it to assign specific tasks to particular study times and sessions. That way, not only do you know when you have time to study, but you also have defined goals for each study session.

Course: _____ Instructor: _____

Date, time, and place of test: _____

Type of test (is it a midterm or a minor quiz?): _____

What the instructor said about the test, including the types of test questions, test length, and how much the test counts toward your final grade:

_____

_____

Topics to be covered on the test, in order of importance (information should also come from your instructor):

1. _____

2. _____

3. _____

4. _____

5. _____

Study schedule, including materials you plan to study (texts, class notes, homework problems, and so forth) and dates you plan to complete each:

MATERIAL   DATE OF COMPLETION

1. _____   _____

2. _____   _____

3. _____   _____

4. _____   _____

5. _____   _____

Materials you are expected to bring to the test (textbook, sourcebook, calculator, etc.):

_____

_____

Special study arrangements (for example, plan study group meetings, ask the instructor for special help, get outside tutoring):

_____

_____

_____

Life-management issues (such as rearranging work hours):

_____

_____

_____

Source: Adapted from Ron Fry, "Ace" Any Test, 3rd ed. Franklin Lakes, NJ: Career Press, 1996, pp. 123–24.

Decide How Well These Techniques Work for You

Now put these studying and scheduling techniques into action by using them every time you prepare for an exam. Make extra copies of the blank checklist so that they're ready to fill out as soon as an exam is announced. After you use these strategies a few times, answer the following questions:

- How did this approach help you organize your time before an exam?

  _____

  _____

  _____

- How did this approach help you organize your study material so that you remembered to cover every topic?

  _____

  _____

  _____

- Can you think of ways to change the checklist to improve your test-prep efficiency? If you can, list the ways here and incorporate them into the checklist.

  _____

  _____

  _____